Developed by
Diane Stortz
with Greg Holder

Most illustrations and some stories
in this book first appeared in variou
volumes of **Easy-to-Teach Bible
Picture Lessons**, © 1994 and 199
by The Standard Publishing Compa
Used by permission.

Scripture in this book is from the
International Children's Bible, New
Century Version, © 1986, 1988 by
Word Publishing, Dallas, Texas
75039. Used by permission.

The Standard Publishing Company, Cincinnati, Ohio. A division of Standex
International Corporation. © 1996 by The Standard Publishing Company.
All rights reserved. Printed in the United States of America.
Library of Congress Catalog Card Number 96-067304.
03 02 01 00 99 98 97 96   5 4 3 2 1

MY Bible Pals™
S T O R Y B O O K

Learning With Friends From the Bible & Today

illustrated by Jodie McCallum

STANDARD PUBLISHING
Cincinnati, Ohio

Table of Contents

Bible Friends

Friends of Today

Bible Friends

Are you ready to hear exciting stories from the Bible? Bible Pals love God and want to do what he says, and the best way to learn is to listen to God's Word, the Bible. So join the Bible Pals now and listen to these stories about Bible friends. You'll be off on an exciting learning adventure!

In the Beginning

Cover your eyes. Long ago, there was no world. No sky, no earth, no people. Everything was dark. Then God said, "Let's make a world," and he did!

First, God made light. *Uncover your eyes.* He made day and night, and earth and sky, and seas and dry ground. God made plants grow. He put the sun and moon and stars in the sky. He filled the seas with fish, and the air with birds.

Then God made all the animals — from the little lady-bug to the very large lion! *Find two ladybugs in the picture. Where is the lion? Can you roar like a lion?*

But God wasn't finished yet. He made the first people — a man named Adam and a woman named Eve. Then God said his world was *very* good! *Clap your hands.*

Talk With Me

• What is your favorite bug? What is your favorite animal?
• Why do you think God made the world?

Say With Me

The Lord God made the earth and the sky. *Genesis 2:4*

Pray With Me

God, I'm so glad you made the wonderful world! I really like
_____ . Thank you for everything you made. Amen.

Ark Full of Animals
from Genesis 6–9

God told Noah to build a BIG boat. "I'm going to send a lot of rain," said God. "You and your family will be safe inside the ark. You will keep animals safe there, too."

Noah obeyed God. *Hammer and saw the wood for the ark.* When the ark was ready, Noah's family went inside. Then God sent animals to the ark, two by two. *"Walk" two fingers into the ark.* Noah helped them all in. Then Noah went inside, too, and God closed the door!

God sent rain for forty days. But everyone on the ark was safe and dry. When the water was gone, Noah and his family and all the animals came out of the ark. And the first thing Noah did was thank God for keeping everyone safe! *Kneel and pray like Noah did.*

Talk With Me

• Name the pairs of animals in the picture.
• What would you like about riding in the ark with Noah?

Say With Me

God said to Noah, . . . "Build a boat." *Genesis 6:13, 14*

Pray With Me

God, you took care of Noah and the animals, and you take care of me. Thank you. I love you, God. Amen.

Baby Isaac's Happy Family
from Genesis 21

Abraham and Sarah had lots of animals. *Moo like a cow. Baaa like a sheep.* They had lots of servants, food, and tents. But there was one thing they did not have. Abraham and Sarah did not have a child, and they wanted one very much. Sometimes they felt very sad because they had grown too old to have any children. *Make a sad face.*

One day three visitors came toward Abraham's tent. The visitors had a message for Abraham — from God! "By this time next year," they said, "Sarah will have a baby."

God always keeps his promises. The very next year, God gave a baby boy to Abraham and Sarah. They named the baby "Isaac," which means "laughter," because they were so happy. *Laugh and make a happy face.*

Talk With Me
• When have you had to wait for something you wanted?
• What has God given you that makes you happy?

Say With Me
Every good . . . gift is from God. *James 1:17*

Pray With Me
Thank you, God, for all the good things you give me. I really like _____ . I love you. Amen.

Joseph's Colorful Coat

from Genesis 37

Jacob was a father who had twelve sons. *Count to twelve.* One son was Joseph. Joseph helped his brothers take care of their father's sheep.

In such a BIG family, you *might* think that no one ever got a special present. But one day, one son *did*. Joseph's father gave him a very colorful coat! Maybe it was striped. Or maybe it had lots of fancy stitching all over. The long sleeves probably helped keep Joseph warm at night.

And when Joseph put on his new coat, maybe he felt as if he were being wrapped up in a BIG hug. *Give yourself a big hug.*

Joseph loved God all his life. I'm sure that Joseph thanked God for his father and for his colorful coat.

Talk With Me

- What is your favorite thing to wear?
- How do feel when you wear it?

Say With Me

The Lord was with Joseph. *Genesis 39:2*

Pray With Me

Thank you, God, for Joseph's colorful coat. I like to hear the stories you put in the Bible. I know they really happened.

Baby in a Basket
from Exodus 1 and 2

God's people, the Hebrews, lived in Egypt. The king of Egypt was afraid of them, so he gave an order. All newborn Hebrew baby boys must be thrown into the river.

But God had a plan. When baby Moses was born, his mother hid him at home for three months. Then she hid him on the river in a little basket. Moses' sister, Miriam, waited to see what would happen. *Pretend you are Miriam, hiding behind the river plants, watching.*

The princess of Egypt came to the river to take a bath. She found Moses in his basket boat. Miriam brought Moses' own mother to help the princess take care of Moses. And when Moses grew up, he helped God's people leave Egypt for a home of their own.

Talk With Me

• Who was looking after Moses? Who takes care of you?
• Who was the helper in this story?

Say With Me

God said, "I will be with you." *Exodus 3:12*

Pray With Me

God, thank you for taking care of me. Even when I'm lonely or afraid, I know you are with me. Amen.

Marching With Joshua
from Joshua 6

Left, right! Left, right! Joshua's army was marching, marching, just as God had told them to do. *March like Joshua's army.* The priests were blowing trumpets, just as God had told them to do. *Pretend to blow your trumpet.*

Around the city of Jericho marched the soldiers and the priests. Joshua led the way. Every day for six days, just as God had said. What a strange way to fight a battle!

Then, on the seventh day, Joshua and the soldiers and the priests marched around the city *seven* times — one, two, three, four, five, six, seven. And on the seventh time, when Joshua called, "Shout!" all the people shouted, and the walls of the city fell right down. *Point to the walls falling down.* God's people won the battle by doing what God said to do!

Talk With Me
- If you were one of the soldiers, how would you feel?
- What is something God has said to do that is hard for you?

Say With Me
The Lord was with Joshua. *Joshua 6:27*

Pray With Me
Dear God, as I grow, please help me learn what you want me to do. Help me to do what you say even when it is hard.

Samuel at the Tabernacle

from 1 and 2 Samuel

Once Hannah was very sad because she didn't have a child. *Make a sad face.* Hannah prayed to God. God gave Hannah a baby boy named Samuel. *Pretend to rock baby Samuel in your arms.*

God had a plan for Samuel! When Samuel was old enough, Hannah brought him to the tabernacle, the place of worship. Samuel stayed at the tabernacle with Eli, the priest, and learned to help Eli with his work. *Sweep the floor. Polish the lamps.* Hannah came to visit Samuel at the tabernacle. Every year she brought him something new to wear.

God blessed Samuel as he grew up, and Samuel became one of God's great servants. He learned to tell God's people what God wanted them to do.

Talk With Me

• How do you think Hannah felt when Samuel was born?
• What would you say to God's people if you were Samuel?

Say With Me

"I have good plans for you." *Jeremiah 29:11*

Pray With Me

God, you planned for little Samuel to grow up and work for you. I'm glad to know you have good plans for me, too!

David Helps the King

from 1 Samuel 16

Out in the fields with his father's sheep, David liked to think about God and play his harp. *Pretend to strum your harp.* David's songs probably made his sheep feel safe and happy, just the way David felt when he thought about God.

But King Saul did not feel safe or happy. His servants thought that music would help him. One servant told the king about David. So King Saul sent a messenger to bring David to the palace.

David played his harp, and the king felt better! *Smile like the happy king.* He asked David to live at the palace. And whenever the king felt sad, David would play his harp to comfort him. *Strum your harp again.*

God was pleased that David had helped the king.

Talk With Me

- What is your favorite musical instrument?
- How can you help someone you know?

Say With Me

Try to learn what pleases the Lord. *Ephesians 5:10*

Pray With Me

Dear God, help me learn what pleases you. Help me learn ways you want me to help other people, too. Amen.

Daniel and the Hungry Lions

from Daniel 6

Daniel was a helper to the king in a faraway land. *Point to Daniel.* Some of the king's other helpers were jealous. They tricked the king into making a new law: "People should pray only to the king." But Daniel prayed to God.

The king's helpers caught Daniel praying to God. Daniel was thrown into a den of hungry lions. *Roar like a lion.* All night the king worried. What would happen to Daniel?

In the morning, the king ran to find out. *Run in place.* There was Daniel, sitting beside the lions! *Sit still like Daniel.* "The lions did not eat me!" called Daniel. "God sent an angel to shut their mouths."

The king set Daniel free. He made a new law, too. "Everyone must worship Daniel's God," said the king.

Talk With Me

• Tell me about a time God kept you safe.
• Do we worship Daniel's God?

Say With Me

Daniel's God is the living God. *Daniel 6:26*

Pray With Me

God, you are so wonderful! You are the only God. Daniel worshiped you, and I want to worship you, too. Amen.

Beautiful and Brave
from the book of Esther

Long ago, a beautiful young girl named Esther became the queen of Persia. The king of Persia did not know that Esther was one of God's people. *Point to Esther. Where is the king?*

One of the king's helpers did not like God's people. *Show me a mad face.* He tricked the king into making a law that would hurt God's people. Who would help them?

Esther was as brave as she was beautiful. She asked God for help. Then she put on her royal robes and went to see the king.

The king was kind to Esther. He listened to her. He made a plan to help God's people instead of hurting them. With God's help, queen Esther had saved her people!

Talk With Me

- Tell me about a time you had to be brave.
- Tell me about a time you asked God for help.

Say With Me

I will not be afraid because the Lord is with me. *Psalm 118:6*

Pray With Me

Sometimes I am afraid, God. When I am afraid, help me remember that you are with me. Amen.

Jonah and the Big Fish
from the book of Jonah

"Go to the city of Nineveh," God said to Jonah. "Tell the people there to stop the bad things they are doing." But Jonah didn't want to go to Nineveh. *Shake your head no.* He ran to the sea and got on a boat. *Where is the boat?*

Then God sent a storm on the sea. The boat was in danger. "I am running away from God," Jonah told the sailors. "Throw me into the sea and the storm will stop." The sailors threw Jonah into the water, and God sent a big fish to swallow him and keep him safe! *Gulp like a big fish.*

Jonah prayed. After three days, God told the fish to spit Jonah out onto dry land. Then God told Jonah to go to Nineveh. This time Jonah obeyed God. The people of Nineveh listened to him, and they obeyed God, too.

Talk With Me

• Tell me about a time you didn't want to obey God.
• What do you think Jonah prayed about inside the fish?

Say With Me

I love the Lord because he listens to my prayers. *Psalm 116:1*

Pray With Me

Dear God, I love you. I know you hear me when I pray, no matter where I am. Thank you for loving me. Amen.

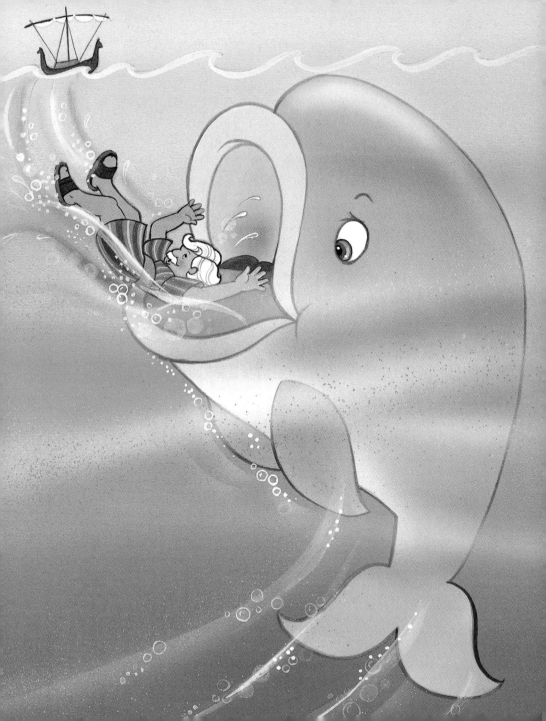

The Savior Is Born
from Luke 2

One quiet night, shepherds were outside guarding their sheep. Suddenly, an angel came, and a bright light shone all around. The shepherds were afraid! *Be a frightened shepherd.*

But the angel said, "Don't be afraid. I have good news for you and for everyone. Today in Bethlehem a baby was born. He is special because he is God's Son. You will find him wrapped in cloths and lying in a manger."

The shepherds hurried into the little town and found baby Jesus lying in a manger, just as the angel had said. *Point to baby Jesus.*

When the shepherds had seen the baby, they told others about what they had seen and heard. Everyone was amazed. Then the shepherds went back to their sheep, praising God.

Talk With Me
• Have you ever seen an angel?
• If you saw baby Jesus, how would you feel?

Say With Me
"Today your Savior was born in David's town." *Luke 2:11*

Pray With Me
Thank you, God, for sending your Son, Jesus, as a little baby. Help me to love and praise him as the shepherds did. Amen.

A Wise Twelve Year Old

from Luke 2

Jesus went to the temple with Mary and Joseph for the first time when he was twelve. *Count to twelve.*

On the long trip home, Mary and Joseph couldn't find Jesus! They hurried back to Jerusalem to look for him.

They looked for three days. Finally, they found him in the temple, talking with the teachers and asking them questions. *Point to the teachers.* He had been there all the time!

Everyone who heard Jesus was amazed at what he knew and how wise he was.

But Jesus had not meant to worry Mary and Joseph. "Didn't you know I had to be in my Father's house?" he said. Jesus went home with Mary and Joseph right away and kept on obeying them.

Talk With Me

• Why did Jesus want to be in the temple?
• Tell me about a time it was hard to obey.

Say With Me

Jesus continued to learn more . . . and to grow. *Luke 2:52*

Pray With Me

Dear God, sometimes it's hard to obey. Help me to be like Jesus. Help me to be wise and to obey. Amen.

Fishermen for Jesus

from Matthew 4

Throw the net, pull the net. Peter and Andrew fished from their boat. *Pretend to throw and pull a big fishing net.* Pull the string, tie the string. James and John were fixing a hole in their fishing net. *Pretend to pull and tie the string.*

Jesus saw Peter, Andrew, James, and John as they worked. He wanted them to be his friends. He knew they would make good helpers. Jesus called to them, "Follow me, and I will show you how to fish for people! You will teach people all about me." *Call the fishermen.*

Peter and Andrew rowed their boat to shore and followed Jesus, just like that! *Pretend to row a boat.* James and John rowed their boat to shore and followed Jesus, just like that! From then on, they were fishermen for Jesus.

Talk With Me

• Let's name some friends that we could tell about Jesus.
• How could we tell these friends about Jesus?

Say With Me

"I will make you fishermen for {people}." *Matthew 4:19*

Pray With Me

Dear God, I want to be like Jesus' fisherman friends and tell tell people all about Jesus. Please help me. Amen.

Down Through the Roof

from Luke 5

A man who couldn't walk had four friends who said, "Jesus can make people well. Let's take our friend to see Jesus!" So they carried the man on his sleeping mat to the house where Jesus was.

But the house was crowded. The friends could not get through the door. They could not get through the windows. So they climbed up to the roof and made a hole in it. *Pretend to climb steps and dig a hole.* Down through the hole they lowered the man on his mat, right in front of Jesus!

Jesus was glad to see the man and his friends. "Stand up," Jesus said. "Pick up your mat and go home."

The man stood up. He was well! Jesus had healed him. The people were amazed, and they praised God.

Talk With Me

- How would you feel if you were the man Jesus healed?
- What are some ways to praise God?

Say With Me

"Today we have seen amazing things." *Luke 5:26*

Pray With Me

Thank you, Jesus, for the wonderful things that you do. I want to always praise you! Amen.

Love One Another

from Matthew 5 and Luke 6

A crowd of people sat on a hillside listening to Jesus talk. *Point to Jesus.* Big people listened. *Find someone big in the picture.* Little people listened. *Find someone little.* People from the town and people from far away listened. Jesus' special helpers listened and others listened, too. *Show me how you look when you are listening.* Everyone wanted to hear about God's love.

Jesus began to teach the people. And the things Jesus taught that day are also for us to learn and live today.

"Love everyone," said Jesus. "Love people who are easy to love and people who are not so nice. Pray for those who treat you badly. God is kind to everyone. He is kind to you. So be kind to others and show them God's love."

Talk With Me

- Do we know anyone who is sometimes hard to love?
- How can we show God's love to that person?

Say With Me

We should show . . . love by what we do. *1 John 3:18*

Pray With Me

Dear God, because you love everyone, I want to love everyone, too. Help me when it's hard. Amen.

A Bumpy Boat Ride

from Luke 8

Jesus got into a boat with his friends and said, "Come with me across the lake." In the boat, Jesus fell asleep. *Shhh, Jesus is sleeping!*

Then big dark clouds came. The wind began to blow. *Blow like the wind.* The waves got bigger and bigger. The boat went up. *Wave your arms up.* The boat went down. *Wave your arms down.* It was a very bumpy ride!

Jesus' friends woke him up. "We're drowning!" they cried.

"Stop blowing," Jesus said to the wind. "Stop crashing," he told the waves. And the wind and the waves were quiet, just like that!

Jesus' friends were amazed. "Even the wind and the waves obey him!" they said.

Talk With Me

- Tell me about a time when you were afraid.
- Tell me about a time when Jesus helped you.

Say With Me

"The wind and the water . . . obey him!" *Luke 8:25*

Pray With Me

Dear Jesus, your power is very great! I know I can trust you to take care of me always. Amen.

Lunch With Jesus
from John 6

One day a crowd was listening to Jesus. Everyone was hungry. *Pat your tummy.* But no one except one small boy had brought any food. The boy had five small loaves of bread *(show me five fingers)* and two small fish *(show me two fingers).* That wasn't nearly enough to feed everyone!

But the boy wanted to share, so he gave his lunch to Jesus. Jesus asked the crowd to sit down. He thanked God for the food. Then he began to break the bread and fish into more and more pieces — until there was enough food for everyone! There was even food left over, enough to fill twelve baskets. *Pretend to pick up leftovers and fill the baskets.*

The people in the crowd were happy, and they were amazed. Jesus, God's Son, has power to do wonderful things!

Talk With Me

• How do you think the boy felt when he gave up his lunch?
• How do you think he felt when he saw what Jesus did?

Say With Me

Be happy to give and ready to share. *1 Timothy 6:18*

Pray With Me

Dear Jesus, help me always to be ready to share whatever I have. Your great power can make my little gifts very big!

Walking on Water
from Matthew 14

After a busy day, Jesus told his friends to get in their boat and go across the lake. *Pretend to row a boat.* Then Jesus went up a hill by himself and prayed all night.

Early in the morning, Jesus was ready to join his friends. It would be a long, long walk to the other side of the lake. There were no cars to drive. *Show me how you would drive a car.* Jesus didn't have a donkey to ride, either. Maybe he could swim. *Show me how you swim.*

But Jesus didn't swim to the boat. Jesus walked on the water. He walked all the way to the boat! "It's a ghost!" cried the disciples.

"Don't be afraid," called Jesus. "It is I." The disciples worshiped Jesus. "You are God's Son," they said.

Talk With Me

• Why is it important for us to pray like Jesus did?
• How do you feel when you think about Jesus' power?

Say With Me

Our Lord is great and very powerful. *Psalm 147:5*

Pray With Me

Jesus, there isn't anyone like you! No one can do the things you do. I want to always love and worship you. Amen.

The Good Neighbor

from Luke 10

Jesus told a story about a man who helped.

Robbers beat up a traveler and took all his money. They left him lying near the road.

A man who worked in God's temple came walking by. *"Walk" two fingers down the road.* But he did not stop to help the hurt man. Then another man came by. *"Walk" two fingers.* But he did not stop, either.

Then a man from another country came. He felt sorry for the hurt man. *Look sad.* He put bandages on all the sore places. He took the hurt man to an inn to rest. And, this man from another country paid for everything himself!

The man who helped was the good neighbor. "I want you to be like the good neighbor," Jesus said.

Talk With Me

• Tell me about a time you have been a good neighbor.
• How do you feel when you help someone else?

Say With Me

Do good to people who need help. *Proverbs 3:27*

Pray With Me

I want to be a good neighbor, God. Show me things that I can do for others who need my help. Amen.

A Special Guest
from Luke 10

When Jesus came to visit, Mary thought he might like to rest. So she invited him to come in and sit down. Mary loved to listen to Jesus. *Show me how Mary sat and listened.*

When Jesus came to visit, Mary's sister Martha thought that Jesus might be hungry and thirsty. She hurried into the kitchen to get things ready. She was very busy. *Show me how Martha cooked and stirred.*

"Jesus," said Martha, "don't you care that Mary isn't helping me? I have so much to do! Tell her to help me."

Jesus smiled. "Martha," he said kindly, "you are worried about making something special for me. But it is more important to hear about God and his love for you. Why don't you sit down and talk with us?"

Talk With Me

• How would you feel if Jesus came to visit at our house?
• What would you do for Jesus if he came to our house?

Say With Me

"You are my friends." *John 15:14*

Pray With Me

Dear Jesus, I am glad to be your friend! Thank you for being my friend. Help me always listen to the things you say.

Talking With God

from Luke 11

Talking with God is called praying. Wouldn't you like to be one of the children in the picture with Jesus, holding his hand and hearing his voice as he prayed? *Which child would you be?* Jesus taught his friends how to pray.

Do we have to talk real loud for God to hear us? No, he hears us even when we whisper. *Let me hear you whisper.* Do we have to be in church to pray? No, God hears us wherever we are. Do we have to close our eyes? No, but sometimes that helps us think about God. *Close your eyes.*

God wants us to tell him what we are thankful for, what we need, what we are sorry about, or what we need help with. God is always listening, whether we have a lot to say or just a little.

Talk With Me

- What are some things you like to talk to God about?
- What are your favorite ways to pray?

Say With Me

God listens to us. *1 John 5:15*

Pray With Me

Dear God, it makes me feel good to know that you are always there to listen to me when I talk to you. Amen.

Thank You, Jesus

from Luke 17

Ten men rested beside a road. They had a terrible skin disease. Doctors could not make them well, and no one wanted them around. This made the men very sad. *Make a sad face.* Who would help them?

Jesus came down the road, and the men called to him. "Jesus! Please help us!"

Jesus wanted to help. He told the men what to do. And as the men began to obey what Jesus said, they were healed! All their sores were gone.

But only one man ran back to Jesus to thank him. *Point to that man.* The other nine ran home. *Point to the others.*

Those nine men made Jesus sad. But the man who said thank-you made him happy! *Make a happy face.*

Talk With Me

• What has Jesus done for you? Have you thanked him?
• What would you say if you were the man who came back?

Say With Me

When you pray, always thank God. *Colossians 4:2*

Pray With Me

God, you do so many good things for me! Help me to always thank you. I love you and I want to do what you say. Amen.

Let the Children Come

from Mark 10

Some mothers and fathers wanted their children to see Jesus. But Jesus' helpers thought Jesus was too busy for that. "Jesus can't see you now," they said. "Don't bother him. You'll have to leave and come back some other time." *Show me how you would stand to keep the mothers and fathers and their children away.*

But when Jesus heard this, he was angry. *Make an angry face.* "Don't send the children away," Jesus said. "Let the children come to me."

The mothers and fathers and children were glad. The children ran to Jesus. Some sat on his lap. Some got a hug. *Give yourself a hug.* Jesus prayed for each child. The mothers and fathers and children were happy. *Make a happy face.*

Talk With Me

• In the picture, which child would you like to be? Why?
• What would you say to Jesus if you could see him?

Say With Me

"Let the little children come to me." *Mark 10:14*

Pray With Me

Dear Jesus, if I could, I would sit on your lap and get a hug and tell you I love you. I'm glad you love little kids like me.

We Want to See!

from Matthew 20

Two men who could not see were sitting beside a road. They heard that Jesus was going by. *Put your hands up to your ears and listen for Jesus.*

The men knew that Jesus could help them. They called to Jesus even though they couldn't see him, "Jesus, Jesus! Please help us, Jesus!" *Call out like these men did.*

And when Jesus came by, he heard the men calling to him from the side of road. He stopped and said, "What do you want me to do for you?"

"We want to *see!*" said the men.

Jesus cared about what these men needed. He touched their eyes. *Touch your eyes.* Right away they could see. They were so happy, and they followed Jesus.

Talk With Me

• What would be hard about not being able to see?
• How would you feel if Jesus healed your eyes?

Say With Me

The Lord has done great things for us. *Psalm 126:3*

Pray With Me

Jesus, your power is very great! Thank you for all the things you do. Help me to always praise you. Amen.

Deciding to Do Right
from Luke 19

Zaccheus was a little man who didn't have any friends, because he cheated people.

One day Jesus came to the town where Zaccheus lived. Zaccheus wanted to see him, but he couldn't see over the heads of the crowd. *Stand on tiptoe.* Zaccheus jumped high. *Jump up and down.* But he still couldn't see Jesus.

So Zaccheus climbed a tree. He looked down. *Look down.* And there was Jesus looking UP at him! *Look up.*

"Zaccheus, come down," said Jesus. "Today I want to stay at your house."

Zaccheus took Jesus to his house for supper. He listened to Jesus' words, and he decided to stop cheating people and do what was good. And Jesus was very happy!

Talk With Me

• Why do you think Jesus wanted to go to Zaccheus' house?
• How would you feel if you were Zaccheus?

Say With Me

Never become tired of doing good. *2 Thessalonians 3:13*

Pray With Me

Dear God, I want to do what is right and good, just like Zaccheus. Thanks for being his friend, and mine, too!

The Palm-Branch Parade

from Matthew 21

Jesus rode into the city of Jerusalem on a donkey. All the people in the city were so glad to see him! Grown-ups and children gathered by the road to watch Jesus ride into town. *Point to the grown-ups. Show me the children. Where is Jesus?*

Some people cut branches from palm trees and waved them to welcome Jesus. *Wave a palm branch.* Others laid their coats in the road so Jesus could ride over them. *Point to the palm branches. Where is the spread-out coat?*

The people were so excited to see Jesus that they began to shout praises to him. "Blessed is the one who comes in the name of the Lord!" they shouted.

It looked like a big parade for Jesus!

Talk With Me

- What do we usually see at a parade?
- Why do you think people were excited to see Jesus?

Say With Me

I will praise you, Lord, with all my heart. *Psalm 9:1*

Pray With Me

God, just like the crowd of people praised Jesus, I want to praise you, too. Thank you for loving me so much. Amen.

An Unselfish Offering

from Mark 12

The temple was a place to worship God. One day Jesus sat down and watched people put their offerings in the money box. *Sit down like Jesus did.*

First many rich people came. They had big purses and poured lots of money into the money box. *Pretend to pour in lots of money.* Their offerings made a lot of noise!

Then a poor woman came into the temple. She had only two little copper coins, worth less than a penny. The two little coins made a tiny little sound — clink, clink — as the woman dropped them into the offering box. *Pretend to drop in coins.*

"That poor woman with the little offering gave more than all the others," Jesus said. "She gave everything she had."

Talk With Me

- Do you have to have a lot of money to give an offering?
- Which person's offering made Jesus happy?

Say With Me

"The way you give to others is the way God will give to you."
Luke 6:38

Pray With Me

Dear God, help me not to be selfish. Help me always be willing to give what I have. I know you'll take care of me. Amen.

God's Precious Promises

from Genesis 9, Luke 2, and Acts 1

God promised Noah that he would never send another flood to cover the whole earth. Then God made a rainbow and put it in the sky. Every time we see a rainbow, we can remember that God loves us. *Pretend to point to a rainbow.*

God promised long ago that someday he would send his Son to earth. Jesus is God's Son! He was born as a little baby. *Pretend to rock baby Jesus.* He grew up to die on the cross for us. But God had also promised that Jesus would live again, and he did!

Then Jesus went back to heaven. His friends didn't want him to leave. But God promised that Jesus will come again and take everyone who loves him to heaven. That will be a happy day! *Clap your hands.*

Talk With Me

- How many promises are in today's story? (Four.)
- What do you think heaven will be like?

Say With Me

"Jesus . . . will come back." *Acts 1:11*

Pray With Me

Dear God, you always keep your promises. I know that Jesus will come back and take everyone who loves him to heaven.

Tell the Good News
from the book of Acts

See the people standing on the dock? Let's count them — one, two, three, four, five, six, seven. Seven men and women and boys and girls. *Where is the baby?* They are all waiting for someone to get off the boat.

Here he comes now! *Point to the man getting off the boat.* His name is Paul. He is a missionary for Jesus. He is going to tell the people the good news about Jesus.

Paul traveled to so many places to tell people about Jesus. Sometimes he traveled by boat. Sometimes he walked. But wherever he went, Paul talked about Jesus. "Jesus loves you," Paul told people. "He died for you. Then God made Jesus alive again, and now he is in heaven. Someday he will come again. This is very good news!"

Talk With Me

• Have you ever told anyone the good news about Jesus?
• Do you know someone who needs to hear the good news?

Say With Me

"Tell the Good News to everyone." *Mark 16:15*

Pray With Me

Dear God, help me be like Paul. I want to tell people the good news about Jesus and his great love. Amen.

Friends of Today

Bible Pals have lots of friends today — children just like you! Every day, children just like you are learning more about God, his world, and his wonderful Son, Jesus! So what are you waiting for? Get ready to start exploring God's Word, the Bible, with these stories of friends of today!

69

The Splish-Splash Day

A story about God's world

What a rainy day! Some of the Bible Pals put on their slickers, boots, and caps and went outside to play in the rain. Lots of little bugs and animals played outside, too. *Hop like a bunny. Crawl like a turtle. Chirp like a bird.*

Richard found a caterpillar who was getting wet and put him on a leaf. *Point to Richard. Point to the caterpillar. What other bugs do you see?*

Nathan dropped pebbles in a puddle and watched the circles that they made. *Where is Nathan?*

Kelsey pointed to the sky and said, "Look at the big bright rainbow!" *Where is Kelsey? Point to the rainbow.*

All the kids thanked God for his beautiful world and their happy splish-splash day!

Talk With Me

• What are some of your favorite rainy-day things to do?
• Name some beautiful things that God made.

Say With Me

This is the day that the Lord has made. *Psalm 118:24*

Pray With Me

Any day is a good day with you, God. Thank you for all the days you give to me. Amen.

Watching Baby Birds
A story about God's world

Marcy liked to watch the birds eat the seeds Mommy put in a bird feeder outside the kitchen window.

Every day one bird flew back and forth to the tree. *Flap your "wings" and fly like a bird.* One day Mommy said, "Look, Marcy! The bird has built a nest right in our tree!" And not long after that, Mommy and Marcy saw three little eggs in the nest. *Hold up three fingers.*

Soon they heard "cheep-cheep-cheep" coming from the nest. *Cheep like a baby bird.* The eggs had hatched! Now there were three little birds in the nest. Marcy watched the mother bird bring food to each of her babies.

"That's how God planned it," said Mommy. "God made all the birds, and he takes care of them, too."

Talk With Me
- Name the colors of the birds in the picture.
- Tell me some things you like about birds.

Say With Me
God . . . made every bird. *Genesis 1:21*

Pray With Me
God, you are very great! You made so many wonderful creatures. Thank you for all the birds you made. Amen.

At the Aquarium

A story about God's world

The daycare class had been learning all week about fish and other underwater creatures. *Put your hands together. Make them swim like a fish.* Then they took a trip in the school minivan to the aquarium.

At the aquarium there were a lot of fish tanks with BIG windows. The fish could look out, and the kids could look in! *Be a fish looking out the window. Be a kid looking in the window.*

"Wow! I didn't know there were so many kinds and colors and shapes and sizes of fish," said Stacy.

"Who made all the fish?" the teacher asked the kids. "Who thought up all those kinds and colors and shapes and sizes?"

"GOD did!" the kids said. "And we're glad he did!"

Talk With Me

- If you were in the picture, which fish would you be? Why?
- Why do you think God made many different kinds of fish?

Say With Me

God . . . created every living thing . . . in the sea. *Genesis 1:21*

Pray With Me

Thank you, God, for all the amazing fish and sea creatures you made. They are fun for us to see! Amen.

Fun in the Sun

A story about God's world

"Let's go to the park today," said Ashley's mom. "Today is a good day for fun in the sun." *Make a big sun with your arms.*

Ashley and her mom went swimming. "Whee! Watch me!" called Ashley as she jumped into the pool.

Nathan and a friend were playing catch. Jenny was going down the slide, and Emily was smelling the flowers. And when the kids got hungry, they could buy snacks at the snack stand. Marcy had a frozen fruit bar the same bright yellow as the sun! *What is your favorite kind?*

"Thanks for taking me to the park," Ashley told her mom that night. "I had a great day. I'm glad God made the sun. I'm glad I could have fun in the sun!"

Talk With Me

• If you were at the park with Ashley, what would you do?
• Tell me some things you like about sunshine.

Say With Me

God made . . . the brighter light to rule the day. *Genesis 1:16*

Pray With Me

I like the warm yellow sun you made, God. Thank you for making it shine for us. I like to have fun in the sun. Amen.

God's Growing Things

A story about God's world

All over David's neighborhood, all through the year, plants grow and change.

In the spring, flowers grow, and people plant gardens. Grass grows, and it's time to start cutting the lawn.

In the summer, vegetables grow. It's fun to eat foods that you grew in your own garden! *Pick some tomatoes.*

Fall is the time for picking apples and for raking up all the leaves when they fall off the trees. *Rake some leaves.* Squirrels are busy storing food for later. They look for acorns that have fallen off the trees. *What would you look like if you were a squirrel with an acorn in your mouth?*

Then it's winter, and God gives a rest to the plants he made. *Be a little plant resting under the snow.*

Talk With Me

• What time of year do you like best? Why?
• If you were in the picture, who would you be? Why?

Say With Me

Everything . . . has its special season. *Ecclesiastes 3:1*

Pray With Me

Dear God, thank you for your wonderful world and all the plants that grow and change. Amen.

A Pet Parade

A story about God's world

Carl liked to stop at the pet store in the mall to see all the animals. There were kittens in the window today. Carl counted them — one, two, three, four, five. Five gray furry kittens. *Find and count the kittens.*

Carl went inside. First he saw the dogs, one brown and one white. *Find the dogs.* A brightly colored parrot in a cage said, "Hello! Hello!" *Say hello like the parrot.* Carl saw bunnies, a hamster, and a guinea pig, too.

Then, because it was pet day, kids began bringing their pets into the mall for a pet parade. Bunnies hopped and fat cats purred and hamsters ran around and around on the wheels inside their cages.

"I'm glad God made so many animals!" said Carl.

Talk With Me

- Tell me about your pet if you have one.
- If you had another pet, what would it be?

Say With Me

God said, "Let the earth be filled with animals." *Genesis 1:24*

Pray With Me

Dear God, you made so many wonderful animals! I am glad for the animals you made for me to enjoy and care for. Amen.

Fun in the Rain
A story about God's world

Tyrone stood at the window and watched the rain. "I wanted to go out and play!" he said. *Make a sad face.*

"You *can* go out and play," said Tyrone's Aunt Deb. "Run and get your coat and boots, and I'll help you put them on." *Make a happy face.*

Tyrone got dressed quickly and ran outside. He had a wonderful time out with the flowers and turtles and ducks and frogs. *Walk like a duck. Jump like a frog.* He listened to the sounds of the rain — kerplop! kerplop! kerplop! He made a little boat and floated it in a puddle.

In a little while, Aunt Deb came out, too. "I like the rain," she said. "God sends it to fall on the earth and help plants and trees and flowers grow." *Grow like a flower.*

Talk With Me

• If you were in the picture, what would you be doing?
• Have you ever played in the rain? What did you do?

Say With Me

"Who sends rain . . . so the grass begins to grow?" *Job 38:27*

Pray With Me

Dear God, thank you for every kind of day you make and every kind of weather you send, even the rain! Amen.

Food From the Farm
A story about God's gifts

Jeremy woke up, yawned, and stretched. *Yawn and stretch.* Today he was going to help Grandpa on the farm!

They fed the chickens and milked the cows. Grandpa let Jeremy ride with him on the tractor, too. *Drive the tractor.* "Our God is a wonderful God, Jimmy," Grandpa said. "He makes food for us." Grandpa pointed to his garden and to the corn in the fields.

In the cow barn, Grandpa said, "God made the cows so we can have fresh milk."

That night after supper, Grandma had a surprise — two big ice cream cones — homemade.

"Our God is wonderful," said Jeremy. "He made the animals, he makes our food, and he gives us ice cream, too!"

Talk With Me

• What are some foods you like? Where do they come from?
• Can you name one food you might like to try?

Say With Me

"Give us the food we need for each day." *Matthew 6:11*

Pray With Me

God, you help us have the food we need and treats like ice cream, too. Thank you for making so many things to eat.

At the Zoo

A story about God's gifts

Beth and her mother went to the zoo on a warm spring day. At the elephant pool, a mother elephant was spraying water all over her baby. *Pretend you're an elephant spraying water with your trunk.* Beth clapped her hands. "That looks like a fun way to get a bath," she said.

To keep cool, Beth and her mother went to watch the dolphins play. The dolphins jumped high into the air and back into the water. "Dolphins like to play in the water just like the elephants do," said Beth.

The dolphin show ended. Beth was thirsty. Mommy helped Beth turn on the drinking fountain. The water tasted good! *Pretend you're getting a drink.*

"I'm glad God gave us water!" said Beth.

Talk With Me

- What are some things you like to do in water?
- What are some things we do with water?

Say With Me

"He gave you water." *Deuteronomy 8:15*

Pray With Me

Dear God, thank you for the water you give for drinking and washing and cooling off. You give us everything we need!

New Shoes for Brett

A story about God's gifts

Brett need new shoes, and he went with his mother to the mall to look for some. *Drive a car to the mall.*

At the shoe store the salesman measured Brett's feet — first the right foot, then the left. *Where is your right foot? Where is your left foot?* Then he said, "Look around the store and find some shoes you'd like to try on."

The first pair Brett chose was a little tight. The second pair was a little loose. But the third pair was just right!

Brett wore his new shoes home. They really helped him run fast and jump high. *Run in place. Jump high.* At dinner that night he showed his new shoes to Daddy. "God is good to us," Daddy said. "He makes it possible for us to have the things we need."

Talk With Me

• What are some things you like about new shoes?
• Tell me about your favorite pair of shoes.

Say With Me

Thank the Lord because he is good. *Psalm 107:1*

Pray With Me

You are really good to me, God! Thank you for giving me all the things I need, even new shoes for running and jumping.

Emily's New Room

A story about God's gifts

When Emily was almost three, her mother said, "Emily, you need a new bed — a big-girl bed! Let's fix up your whole room, too!" So Emily and her mother went shopping. They found a new bed, a comforter with Emily's favorite colors, wallpaper and paint, and a little shelf.

Emily's mother and father worked hard, painting and papering the walls. Emily helped. *Paint pretend walls.* When the work was done, Emily's daddy put her new bed together, and Emily's mother put on the sheets and the new comforter. Emily put her favorite toys on the new shelf.

Now Emily's room was so cozy! Emily turned on her angel night-light and thanked God for her new room. *Fold your hands and bow your head.*

Talk With Me

- What are some things you like about our house?
- How many different kinds of homes can you think of?

Say With Me

"Your Father knows the things you need." *Matthew 6:8*

Pray With Me

God, thank you for my home and my own warm bed. Thank you for knowing what I need and giving me what I need.

The New Neighbor

A story about God's gifts

Jonathan watched the moving van back into the driveway next door. *Show me how you would drive a moving van.* Would the new family have any kids his age?

Soon a car pulled up. A man, a woman, and a girl got out. The girl used a wheelchair. She waved at Jonathan. *Wave hello.* Jonathan walked over and said hi. The girl's name was Brittany.

Brittany was glad to have a friend. She couldn't run, but she could catch and throw a ball. And she liked to go for walks in her chair. She let Jonathan push her to the corner and back, even though she could do it by herself.

Now the new neighbor on Jonathan's street was a new friend, too!

Talk With Me

- Why is it important to be friendly to new people you meet?
- What is the best thing about having a friend?

Say With Me

Dear friends, we should love each other. *1 John 4:7*

Pray With Me

Thank you, God, for all my friends. Help me be a friend to everyone I meet, because you love us all. Amen.

Fun With Daddy
A story about God's gifts

Kelsey's daddy had to go away for a week on a business trip. He gave Kelsey a big hug and said, "I'll be home soon. Help Mommy and remember to thank God for taking care of our family every day." Kelsey waved good-bye as Daddy got on the airplane. *Wave good-bye.*

All week long Kelsey helped her mother as Daddy had asked. Every day she asked God to take care of her family.

Then Saturday came and Daddy was home! He brought Kelsey a new ball. "I promised to teach to you catch," Daddy said. "We'll practice today." *Pretend to throw and catch a ball.*

Kelsey had fun with Daddy. She was so glad for the family God had given her!

Talk With Me
• Why do you think God gives kids mommies and daddies?
• Tell me some ways that you have fun with your daddy.

Say With Me
"Honor your father and your mother." *Deuteronomy 5:16*

Pray With Me
Thank you, God, for all the people in my family. Thank you for giving us families to live in. Help me love my family, too.

Fun at Church

A story about God's gifts

Today was Leisha's first day in her new Sunday school class. She looked around the big room. Everything was different. Leisha felt very alone. *Show me a sad face.*

Miss Ellen, Leisha's new teacher, was carrying a big red box. "Leisha," called Miss Ellen, "would you help me open my box?"

Leisha opened the box. Inside were stuffed animals and puppets! Miss Ellen handed Leisha a fuzzy lamb.

The children sang songs, and Miss Ellen told a story about God and all the animals he made.

"I like my new teacher and my new class!" Leisha said.

"Yes," said Miss Ellen. "Church is a happy place to be." *Clap your hands.*

Talk With Me

• What makes our church a happy place?
• Is there anything you would change about our church?

Say With Me

You are chosen people. *1 Peter 2:9*

Pray With Me

Dear God, I like to go to church! Thank you for all the people there who love you and teach me all about Jesus. Amen.

Daddy's Bible

A story about God's gifts

Josh went to Grandpa's house while his mother went to a meeting. Grandpa had lots of toys to play with. And he told Josh stories about Josh's daddy when he was little!

Grandpa made some hot cocoa and cookies. *Pretend to drink cocoa and eat cookies.* Josh sat at the table and told Grandpa all about school. Then Grandpa brought out a box. "I've been saving this for you," he said. Inside was a Bible with lots of pictures. It was Josh's daddy's Bible when he was a boy! *Pretend to turn the pages of the Bible.*

Grandpa read Josh the story of Jesus and the children. "That's my favorite," said Josh.

"The Bible is God's special book," said Grandpa. "Let's thank him right now!"

Talk With Me

• Show me your Bible. What is your favorite Bible story?
• Let's look at the pictures in your Bible.

Say With Me

You know that these teachings are true. *2 Timothy 3:14*

Pray With Me

Thank you, God, for your special book, the Bible. Help me to learn what you say there and to do what you say. Amen.

The Looking Day

A story about what I can do

Monica's looking day began when she got up and looked for something to wear. She chose her red and white dress, her white socks with a red stripe, and her tan shoes with a button on the strap. *Point to Monica's dress, socks, and shoes.*

Then Monica looked for something to eat. Her mother helped her find cereal, juice, and milk in the kitchen.

Then Monica looked for something to do. She found her puppy to play with in the backyard, and she chased a yellow butterfly that fluttered by. *Pretend to chase a butterfly.*

Then Monica said, "I looked for something to wear, I looked for something to eat, and I looked for something to do. I'm glad God gave me eyes so I can look!"

Talk With Me

- Tell me about some of your favorite colors.
- What are some other things you like to see?

Say With Me

I praise you because you made me. *Psalm 139:14*

Pray With Me

Thank you, God, for my eyes that can see, and for all the wonderful things you made for me to see. Amen.

The Listening Day

A story about what I can do

When Nathan is very tired, he likes to take a nap. But when he wakes up, he likes to use his ears to listen to all the sounds around him. *Show me your ears.*

Nathan can hear music. Sometimes he hears music on the radio. Sometimes he hears his sister, Bridgett, practicing the piano. *Where is Bridgett?* He hears his dog, Tippy, barking. *Where is Tippy?* He hears a bird outside singing happy chirping songs. *Point to the little bird.*

Nathan can hear the people he loves. He hears his mother singing songs about God's love. *Show me Nathan's mother.* He hears his baby brother crying. *Find the baby.* He hears the familiar voice of the weather reporter on TV.

Nathan is glad God made ears so we can hear!

Talk With Me

- Name some sounds you like to hear.
- Name some sounds you like to make. Make them now.

Say With Me

I praise you because you made me. *Psalm 139:14*

Pray With Me

Thank you, God, for making me with ears that can hear. Thank you for all the wonderful things there are to hear.

The Tasting Day

A story about what I can do

At the fair, Sarah laughed and screamed on the roller coaster. Brett smiled and waved as his merry-go-round horse went up and down. *Smile and wave.* And Ashley took a ride on a real pony. Giddyap! *Gallop like a pony.*

For lunch, everyone got a hot dog, french fries, and pop. Brett put ketchup on his hot dog. Sarah put mustard on hers. Ashley put ketchup *and* mustard on hers.

"Time for dessert!" said Sarah's mother. Brett got a cold, creamy chocolate ice cream cone. Sarah got cotton candy, sweet and sticky. And Ashley got salty popcorn.

It was a fun and yummy day! The three friends were glad God gave them mouths to taste hot and cold, creamy and crunchy, and salty and sweet.

Talk With Me

- What are your favorite things to eat?
- Name some salty foods. Name some that are sweet.

Say With Me

You made me in an amazing . . . way. *Psalm 139:14*

Pray With Me

Thank you, God, that I can taste all the wonderful foods that are in the world you made. Amen.

The Feeling Day

A story about what I can do

When Leisha and Maria went to the fair, their favorite place was the petting zoo. The little white lamb's woolly coat felt soft. The lamb let Leisha hug him! *Give yourself a hug.*

The turtle was lying on the ground with his head and feet inside his shell. He was very sleepy. *Rub your eyes as if you are very sleepy.* Maria carefully picked him up. He slowly put his head out and blinked his little black eyes. He put out his feet and little tail. *Wake up like the little turtle.* Maria put the turtle back on the ground to finish his nap. His shell felt hard and bumpy.

Two other animals the girls saw were the alligator and the porcupine. You might not want to pet those two! But what do you think they might feel like if you could?

Talk With Me

- What are your favorite things to touch and feel?
- Name some other textures besides hard and soft.

Say With Me

You made me in an amazing . . . way. *Psalm 139:14*

Pray With Me

Thank you, God, that I can touch and feel so many different things. You made me in an amazing and wonderful way.

The Smelling Day
A story about what I can do

Jeremy and Jenny and their cousin Brock visited Grandpa's farm. The hay in the barn smelled good. The cows didn't smell quite as good. *Hold your nose.* And the skunk in Grandma's garden did not smell nice at all! *Hold your nose and shake your head.*

The children went to tell Grandpa about the skunk. They passed the big apple tree, covered with blossoms. That smelled good! Jenny stopped to smell a flower. *Pretend to smell a flower like Jenny did.* "Flowers smell a lot better than farm animals!" Jenny laughed.

Then Jeremy and Jenny smelled one of Grandma's apple pies. "I'm glad God made our noses so we can smell things," said Joshua. "I wouldn't want to miss eating that pie!"

Talk With Me
- What are some of your favorite things to smell?
- What is one way that bad smells can help us?

Say With Me
What you have done is wonderful. *Psalm 139:14*

Pray With Me
Dear God, with my nose I can smell all the smells in the wonderful world you made. Thank you for making me! Amen.

Playing in the Park
A story about what I can do

Playing in the park is fun! David climbs to the top of the tower. He turns the steering wheel and pretends to fly a big jet plane. *Fly the plane with David.*

Richard and Brett climb up the ladder to the slide. Brett goes down first. Beth and some other kids in the group go down through the tunnel. Whee! *Pretend to climb up. Pretend to slide down.*

Monica and Jonathan like to run across the swinging bridge. *Pretend to run across the bridge.*

Austin and Rhonda think riding a bike and skating are fun things to do at the park, too.

It's great to run and play with the wonderful arms and legs God gave to you!

Talk With Me
- Which child in the picture would you like to be?
- Tell me some things you like to play outside.

Say With Me
What you have done is wonderful. *Psalm 139:14*

Pray With Me
Thank you, God, for the body you made for me. Thank you for all the things my body can do. Amen.

Learning is Fun

A story about what I can do

Carl likes to go to preschool. There are lots of things to do, and lots of friends to play with. And Carl likes to learn.

He is learning his colors — red, yellow, blue, and green. *Find each color in the picture.* Sometimes he has trouble remembering yellow, but that's OK. He's learning.

Carl is learning to count — one, two, three, four, five. *Show me five fingers. Can you count higher than that?* Sometimes he forgets what comes after three, but that's OK. He's learning.

Today Maria asked Carl to play a game with her, with Richard, and with Sarah. Carl knew his colors, and he could count on the board. Everyone took turns and everyone had fun. Carl thanked God for making him so he could learn!

Talk With Me

• Tell me some things you have been learning.
• What are some things you would like to learn more about?

Say With Me

Lord, . . . you know all about me. *Psalm 139:1*

Pray With Me

Thank you, God, that I can learn. Help me as I learn. Thank you for all the wonderful things there are to understand.

God Made Me Special

A story about what I can do

Stacy peeked through the door at Sunday school. Beau was lying on a big sheet of paper, and Miss Thomas was drawing around him. That looked like fun! Miss Thomas drew around Stacy, too. Then Beau and Stacy colored their pictures. *Where is Beau's picture?* "God made each one of you very special," said Miss Thomas.

Juan's canary was singing for everyone to hear. Stacy loved to sing, too. She found her favorite instrument to play, the tambourine. Then she sang "Jesus Loves Me" while she played the tambourine. *Sing "Jesus Loves Me." Play an instrument if you have one. What other instruments are in the box?* Stacy was happy God had made her special and she could sing to him.

Talk With Me

- Tell me something special about you.
- Tell me something special about a friend.

Say With Me

Lord, . . . you know all about me. *Psalm 139:1*

Pray With Me

God, I know that there is no one else just like me, and you made me. You love me and I love you. Amen.

Thanking God for Parents

A story about God's care

Carl had a headache and a fever. His mother brought him a drink of water, and his father went to the store to get some medicine. While he waited, Carl looked outside. *Look all around.*

Everywhere he looked, he saw mothers and fathers and their kids. One family was going to the park. Another family was getting ready for a picnic in their yard.

Monica's dad was helping her learn to ride her two-wheeler. Kelsey and her mom were jogging. *Jog in place.* And Jeff's dad was rescuing Jeff's cat from a big tree. *Meow.*

"Here's your medicine," Carl heard his dad say.

"Thanks, Dad!" said Carl. "I sure am glad God gave kids moms and dads to take care of them!"

Talk With Me

• What do you like to do with your mom and dad?
• What do you like your mom and dad to do for you?

Say With Me

Children are proud of their parents. *Proverbs 17:6*

Pray With Me

Thank you, God, for parents. Thank you for my mom and dad and all the things they teach me and do for me. Amen.

Thanking God for Friends
A story about God's care

Beau was lonely. His best friend, Todd, had started going to school, but Beau could not go to school until next year. *Make a lonely face.* "I miss Todd," Beau told his mom.

"I know you feel sad," she said. "Todd is still your friend. But we will ask God for a new friend for you, too."

The next day Beau and his mom went to Bible study. Beau played in the playroom. A new boy, Alex, was there. Beau and Alex had fun together! *Point to Beau and Alex.*

When it was time to go home, Alex's mother asked if Beau could go home with Alex for the afternoon. Beau's mother said yes. Beau had a great time at Alex's house.

That night Beau prayed, "Thank you, God, for giving me a new friend — Alex!"

Talk With Me
- Who are your good friends? Why are they your friends?
- What are some things friends like to do together?

Say With Me
A friend loves you all the time. *Proverbs 17:17*

Pray With Me
Thank you, God, for giving me friends. Help me to treat them nicely. Help me to make new friends, too. Amen.

Thanking God for Church
A story about God's care

Jenny's Sunday school teacher greeted her at the door. "What would you like to do today?" she asked.

Jenny looked around. Jeremy was singing. Kelsey and Nathan were coloring. Leisha was looking at the Bible. Maria was working a puzzle. Richard was trying to make his fingers look like the church building in the puzzle. *Point to all of Jenny's friends at church.*

Then Jenny thought about the home living center. "I want to find a doll," she said.

Jenny brought her doll over to watch Maria work her puzzle. "I like to come to church," Jenny told her teacher.

"Thank you, God, for church," the teacher said. "It's a happy place to be."

Talk With Me

• What do you like to do when you go to church?
• Tell me about some of your friends at church.

Say With Me

Your people meet to worship you. *Psalm 22:22*

Pray With Me

Thank you, God, for church. Thank you for my friends there and the happy times we have together, learning about you.

Thanking God for Helpers
a story about God's care

Nathan and his mom drove into town. "Count the helpers that you see," said Nathan's mom.

First, Nathan counted Matt, the grocery store clerk, who helped load the car. Second, Nathan counted the police officer directing traffic and helping people cross the street safely. *Point to Matt. Point to the police officer.*

A doctor and his nurse talked about how to help a patient get well. Now Nathan had counted four helpers. *Point to the doctor and nurse.*

Two firefighters cleaned the fire truck and waited for the next alarm. That made six helpers. *Find the firefighters.* The mail carrier made seven helpers all together. *Find the mail carrier.* "I'm glad God made so many helpers," said Nathan.

Talk With Me

- Which helper in the picture would you like to be? Why?
- What are some things that helpers have done for you?

Say With Me

He cares for you. *1 Peter 5:7*

Pray With Me

Thank you, God, for all the jobs people do that help me and others. Thank you for taking care of me always. Amen.

FOOD MARKET

Thanking God for Pets

A story about God's care

Tyrone knocked on Miss Jane's door. Miss Jane had a dog named Daisy who was going to have puppies soon! Tyrone gave Daisy a drink. He sat on the floor and gently rubbed her ears.

"I am thankful God made dogs," said Miss Jane. "Daisy is a nice dog, and she is good company for me."

The next time Tyrone visited Miss Jane, she met him at the door and said, "Close your eyes." She led him into the kitchen. When Tyrone opened his eyes, he saw Daisy with little furry puppies! *Point to Daisy. Count the puppies.*

"I asked your mother if you may have one of the puppies when they are old enough to leave their mother," said Miss Jane. "She said yes, you may!" *Clap your hands.*

Talk About It

- Do you like pets? What is good about having pets?
- What do we do to take care of our pets?

Say With Me

The earth is full of the things you made. *Psalm 104:13*

Pray With Me

Thank you, God, for puppies and kittens and fish and all kinds of animals for us to care for and love. Amen.

I'm Growing Up!

A story about God's care

Jeff and his big brother, Austin, were getting ready for church. Jeff put on his light blue shirt. The buttons wouldn't button. *Pretend to try to button.* Jeff pulled on his dark blue pants. The pants wouldn't snap, and Jeff could see the tops of his socks. What was wrong? *Pretend to try to snap pants.*

Austin tried to button Jeff's shirt. He tried to snap Jeff's pants. "I think I know what has happened," said Austin. "You have grown!"

Jeff was surprised. He didn't feel taller.

"Let's measure you," said Austin. Sure enough, Jeff had grown *three* inches!

"Now I'll be tall enough to reach the football on the top shelf!" said Jeff. "I'm glad God is helping me grow!"

Talk With Me

• Are you growing? How do you know?
• What are some things you want to do when you are bigger?

Say With Me

Surely your . . . love will be with me all my life. *Psalm 23:6*

Pray With Me

Thank you, God, that I am growing up. Help me to love you more and more every day of my life. Amen.

There are many other **Bible Pals** products for you and your young children to enjoy!

Look for these at your favorite Christian bookstore.

My Bible Pals Spinner Games (28-02657), features a built-in spinner and six easy-to-play board games that teach Bible values. Play by color — no reading or counting required!

Four tall, sturdy board books teach the lives of important Bible characters and educational concepts, too!
>   **My Name Is David: Fun With Colors (24-03447)**
>   **My Name Is Moses: Fun With Words (24-03449)**
>   **My Name Is Noah: Fun With Shapes (24-03450)**
>   **My Name Is Jesus: Fun With Counting (24-03448)**

Two different 16-page coloring books, each with Bible-story pictures and modern-day pictures.
>   **Bible Friends (23-22009)**
>   **Jesus & Me (23-22010)**

My Bible Pals Stickers. Two different books, each with 36 self-stick designs.
>   **Kids 'n Jesus (22-01017)**
>   **Kids 'n Bibles (22-01018)**